Queen of Broken Hearts
and Waterfall Tears

For those that struggled in the year that we all wish never was. Remember that we all get stronger once we get back up again. Dust off your shoulders and try again. And if all fails, write a book about it!

Contents

Spring

March 4, 2020

I am falling through the air
Cold air whipping at my face
And tossing my hair above me
A parachute too weak to save me
My face emotionless as I gasp
No scream in my throat
Seconds away from breaking
Yet hidden so far behind a mask
I do not know how to save myself
I'm better off crashing
Letting the waves surround me
And crash over my body
Until it burns
Sinking me into darkness
I'm better lost
Crashing
Breaking
Smashing
Just like I always do
To save them

March 21, 2020

My bones ache as I awake
From a dream I barely remember
Breaking as I fall further and further
Trying to call out yet hearing nothing
I wonder
Why do I feel so odd
I usually love to create and talk
But lately, I can barely walk
So I hide behind a smile
And type afraid to fall
To fall behind
To fall deeper into my mind
This morning I was excited to be here
But then after something so small
My feelings aren't so clear
I have lost my creativity
But that is fine with me
So I hide behind a smile
Too afraid to fall
To fall behind
To lose the friends that
Are blind
To my fears
Of silence
Of being forgotten
If I take one day to just
Do nothing

So I fake my smile
All the while
I am numb inside

March 25, 2020

I am sorry if we used to talk every hour of the day
And now you wait for me to reply
I am here to tell you why
I am falling,
Crushed beneath the struggle of online schooling
My assignments pile up
And I crumble into anxiety
I try to respond to as many people as I can
As I stumble in this strange new wonderland
But still, I fall again and again
I don't mean to leave you without a reply
But I am one person and I haven't yet been able to
Fly … past this struggle
I fear you hate me, I fear that my silence has caused
The same loneliness I feel every day
But just know I am not ignoring you
I will talk too
Just give me some time to adjust
Because I do think of you, every day
Always worried that I cannot keep up and worried
You'll get bored of me and fade away

April 13, 2020

I am losing control
Always on the verge of tears
Yet never having the relief of crying
Sinking
Falling
No control
Control freak
Freak that needs control
I wish I could
I'm sorry I can't
Leave
Never come back
Yet too attached to fade away
Control freak
Not in control

April 15, 2020

We accept the love we think we deserve
We take the roses soaked in black
Tainted by decayed water, and paint them red
We wrap bubble gum around our hearts
And let them pop it like a balloon
We accept the love we think we deserve
We accept nothing
Yet we are blind to it all

April 17, 2020

I struggle to float when the water submerges me
Silently crying out for help
Thrashing
Choking
Dying
Under the weight of a million voices

Yet when the water is barren
I cry
For the voices have gone too
And where there was death
There was also life

Now both are missing

April 20, 2020

I'm so frustrated right now
They twist words
And chain my wrists to a keyboard
Why did I think this was a good idea
I should have given up
I should have known
I would fail
To be human

April 20, 2020

Funniest part is
I don't know who I am trying to impress
I digress
Rant the words that drown me inside
Mental suicide
Not my parents cause they aren't hard on me
I think I need psychology
Please don't leave
I need to grieve
But I'm moving too fast to function

You need to take it slow,
you're just going to end up feeling low.
Try to take time for yourself.
Put the work on a shelf,
just take a pause,
a mental breakdown is something you don't want
to cause.
So take a break,
everything will be okay.
-L

April 23, 2020

The world cursed me
Drained words that let me see
The happiness that let me be
And all that remains is absentee
Why is that when I am sinking
People reply before my eyes?
Yet without fail
When I am free
To be me
And my eyes clear to see
There are no replies waiting for me?

April 24, 2020

I feel rude
Is it crude to be so optimistic
I roll my eyes
Petrified that my silence is permitted
Because when I speak
I know I'll squeak
About the fact that it may not happen
So here I sit
My mind filled with shit
About rainbows
And "You don't know yet"

April 25, 2020

I miss you
Every time I am blind
It makes me blue
For when it comes to what you do
No one is finer
I wish you
would let me see again
Yet all I do is let the tears shed
Because I never truly see you
Not yesterday
Not today
And probably never again

May 1, 2020

Cancel or Discard
All you do is watch from a distance
Yet for some reason
It makes the tears fall from my face
It feels like I am mute
Like no one can hear me
Cancel me
Or discard me
Either way
You are ignoring me
And it hurts

May 2, 2020

I am bored
I am sad
And I'm also kinda glad
That it is almost time to sleep
Cause when I awake
It is great (Give or take)
Cause everyone talks to me
I admit
I'm a twit
Cause I act like silence doesn't bother me
But it does
And it's cause
I feel ignored and lonely

May 11, 2020

You spend the money to buy good fireworks
Yet they left you
Without a spark to make the colors burst
Leaving you empty
And with a hole where the colors might have been

They spend nothing
And find just the right spark
To light the night sky

You try to be happy and watch
As their fireworks sparkle and crack
Yet you cannot help but cry

Selfish
Selfless
Selfish
Selfless

A never-ending game
Of caring about your own stupidity
Or their success

May 12, 2020

No one is online
I am bored outta my mind
I would try to fall asleep
But I can't, so I weep
I try to distract the thoughts in my head
Telling me they hate me so I am misled
I keep clicking back waiting to see more than 'sent'
But there isn't a change and now here I vent

May 13, 2020

Copy and paste you say ...
Do you mean like your fake smile
That you share with everyone?
Do you mean like your keynote presentation
That was mostly quotes?
Or the movies you downloaded
Off of a dodgy website?
You call yourself a teacher
But I put in more hard work
Thank you

May 14, 2020

I want to let you live
To share all that you can give
I want to be supportive
But it makes me uncomfortable and distorted
I do not like it so I delete it discreetly
But isn't that the same as lying concretely
I'm sorry it makes me feel all odd
But could please stop sharing --

Mat 14, 2020

Paint my ears blue
And block out the sounds
So I never hear you
Stick glue between my teeth
And fill in the spaces
So I can never speak again
Then stab my eye with a paintbrush
Until it bleeds into blackness
So I can never see the pain again

Mar 20, 2020

One happy day
Is too much to say
How is it that a place that brought smiles
Now leaves me in a state of denial
I say I'm fine
But clearly, it is a lie
I smile and color
But motherfucker
something comes once again to sour my mood
So you know what
Just erase me
Ah the memory

May 21, 2020

Social visiting is not the same
As social distancing
Just because they rhyme
Does not make it fine
To go out and have a party
You aren't careful
I am despairful
At the idiocy within you
It would be great
If you would just wait
To have a house full of people

May 27, 2020

Will I be sleep deprived
Out of my mind
When what I feel inside
Makes me feel twisted and tied
Like lava is melting
Welting
My skin in pieces

I hate having heat inside my veins
If I could be cold blooded
I would move into that lane
Because this is annoying

Summer

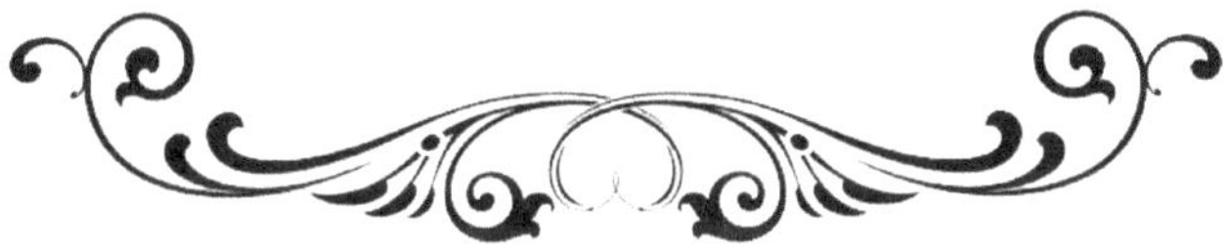

June 1, 2020

I keep clicking
At the speed time is ticking
Waiting for a conversation
I already know will not happen
Listening to songs as my nails are tappin
Not caring about the song
Because I care more that this is taking too long
Because I have nothing else to do
But wait for you

June 1, 2020

Red is rage
Red is blood
Red is forever
Red is love

June 2, 2020

Red is the blood that never bled
Red is her lips so sweet against my own
Red is the passion of love
And the rage of a nation
Red is everyone, everything
It is everywhere

June 3, 2020

Red is stop
Red is no
Red is fight
Red is woe
It depends on what you see
It can be evil
It can be kind
But through it all
We have to mind

June 4, 2020

Orange is summer
Orange is sweet
Orange can be evil
It isn't too hard a feat

June 5, 2020

Orange is hands entwined
As her eyes peer in mine
Orange is cautionary
Orange is a burst of sunrise
Between my teeth
Orange is good and bad
Orange is every moment, everywhere

June 5, 2020

I try to reach out
To explain why I pout
But then they have nothing to say
I wonder if I am hated
All day I waited
But still nothing ... so I cried

June 6, 2020

Orange is sunset
Orange is bad guy
Orange is sunkissed
Orange is a lie
But through it all
We have to try

June 7, 2020

Yellow is caution
Yellow is blind
Yellow is school
Changing the mind

June 8, 2020

Yellow is the joy in their eyes
As laughter fills their mouths
Yellow is slow down
Yellow is warning
Caution
Yellow is lemons
Sour or sweet
Depending on who you ask
Yellow is
Good
Bad
Ugly
And adorable
Yellow is everything

June 9, 2020

Yellow is the sun in the sky
Yellow is slow down
Yellow is refreshing
Yellow is sour frown
In the towns
Where we all drown
So instead of being stupid
We need to come around

June 10, 2020

Green is spring
Green is new
Green is greed
Green is you

June 11, 2020

Green is the feeling of their arms around me
Lips lighting my body with new life
Like a garden
Green is the greed of evil idiots
And selfish pricks
Green is sickness I feel
When I see their acts
Green is go, but not for everyone
Green is living
So live it

June 12, 2020

Green is need to go
Green is how they make me sickly
Green is dough
Need to end this shit quickly

June 13, 2020

Blue is the sky so calm
Blue is the tears cried
Blue is peace never achieved
Blue is how hard we never try

June 14, 2020

Blue is his hands pulling me closer
Blue is the sky so calm and clear
Blue is morality spoken aloud for all to hear
Blue is the pain worse than heartbreak
Blue is sadness
Blue is happy
Blue is every emotion
Including sappy

June 14, 2020

Silence comes as all things do
In the calm dark of night
Yet the night is more complex than the light
It has more color and more sound
But the insanity of being silent drowns
It all out
I wish that quietness would not overtake me
When I have nothing to do but see
The bare walls
Yet when I want to just let be
I am overcome by the craziness of words
Like a flock of birds
Trying to capture me
Silence is more complex than sound
Because with silence comes
The overwhelming yells
Of the dangerous bells
Of the loneliness
Inside me

June 15, 2020

Blue is ice, piercing, and sharp
Blue is kind like a golden heart
Blue is eyes, bubbling and crying
Blue is the part where we have to restart
Because an old man tore it apart

June 16, 2020

Indigo is loneliness seeping in
Indigo is logic in the face of idiocy
Indigo is space
Indigo is tears, treated so hideously

June 16, 2020

Radio silence
A saying so bold
Yet nothing is silent
So ignore what's told
About silence being quiet

Radios speak loud
And so does my head
It shouts like a rowdy crowd
While I sit in my bed

I wish people would speak
To me
Instead of just letting me free
To be radio silenced

June 16, 2020

When I am busy, they give me everything
The world is perfect
When I have nothing, they give me nothing
The world is unfair
I would trade my soul
For a life where
I have nothing and am given everything
But that was never a choice

June 16, 2020

Loneliness is my new best friend
We dance across the sea of green
Around the willow tree
Where flower petals of
Of new buds had died
To give our feet a softer landing

Loneliness with her sad blue eyes
Kisses me with frostbitten lips
Chapped from the salt in her tears
Goodbye
Farewell
She sings in a tone that is both quiet
Yet somehow deafening in my ears

But she is never saying goodbye to me
Just to the friends I've not met yet
And to the people that fell away
Like the buds wilting on the willow tree
Like the tears we once cried together

June 17, 2020

Ten

Ten days away I say

Counting down
As I decay
My birthday
Only so far away
It will be my last year
to be a teen
And gloat and cheer
To be twenty I do fear
But I still got another year
Until I'm no longer
A teen

19

in 10

9

8 …

June 17, 2020

My blood flows through my body
Like an invisible river
For no one to see
My heart beats faster
All the voices in my mind
Calling out across the line
They scream at me
That this was how it was meant to be
As the river flows stronger
Your words
Breaking down the barrier
And releasing a heart beating
They tell me when it kicks in
And all the sides agree
That you are where I should be

June 17, 2020

Indigo is his words wrapped around my heart
As our tongues meet together
Indigo is
Depression, Repression, Regression
Indigo is learning new things
And teaching who needs to be taught
Indigo is speaking loudly for all to hear
Indigo is every thought, on every tier, everywhere

June 18, 2020

Indigo is shyness
Indigo is frustration, not being heard
Indigo is brokenhearted
Indigo is flipping the bird

June 19, 2020

Violet is voices shouting
Violet is blood pumping through veins
Violet is a mysterious haze
Violet is history stains
Written by the white man
And in need of fixing

June 19, 2020

Loneliness finds me again
My only friend once more
As the sun paints shadows
Across the bleary sky
She whispers in my ear
Secrets that must never be spoken
Yet all I hear is lies swirling off the tip
Of her incessant tongue
She tells me that they
Have better things to do
That they have a family
A life
But why does it feel
Like they are fading
Falling further
From my outstretched palm
She stabs me with words
So shining and bright
That they burn my body
I know that lives are better
Real than fake
But don't you realize
That it is my only
Distraction to the destruction
At every dawn of a new day
I need you
Like I need water

A headache coming
When my thirst is not quenched
As the tears fill my eyes
Yet again

June 20, 2020

The silence hurts
Only an hour without you
Breaking me into pieces
When your voice ceases
Stuck checking my phone too
Trying to see if it is just the internet
You say don't sweat it
But I do
Because you are my only friend
When the moon comes in view
So as the tears fall
Dripping down my face
I can't help but ask if the space
Is on purpose
Or if I
am who you hate

June 20, 2020

The princess looks out at the waterfall
Watching the water slide down into the abyss
She sees them in the reflection
The Princes and the Queens disguised as royalty
And they had hurt her
Until not even her heart knew what it wanted
She stepped through the water
Trying to get a better look
To try and see where she had gone wrong
Yet what she found
Were her hands entwined with another
Looking up into the eyes of a kinder soul
He smiled down at her
And she saw her reflection, so she reflected
On what she knew
She had been rescued
And she had found love
Where she thought there would be none
He had shown her her heart
She loved him
Love whispers to her at night
Overlapping with the screams of loneliness
Until love is the winner
Love holds her softly
Promises never to let go
Love is him
Always, Forever

June 20, 2020

Violet is her gentle grip on my hand
His hips against me
And them kissing my lips all at once
Every gender
Violet is the calm after the storm
Violet is imperfect perfection
Never touched or rewritten
Yet deserves to be burned
Violet is nonviolent calm
Yet they claim violence
Is all it will be
As you click through the tragedy
Violet is playing princess
When all you ever wanted to be
Was the Prince
Violet is every word
Every meaning, everywhere

June 22, 2020

Rainbow is happiness
Rainbow is gay
Rainbow is inclusion
Rainbow is every he, ze, she, and they

June 23, 2020

Rainbow is her lips against my own
His hands in mine
And their arms holding me close
Rainbow is letting everyone be free
Rainbow is not judging who someone wants to be
Rainbow is love, Rainbow is strong
Fighting for human rights all day long
Rainbow is smiles, Rainbow is gay
Love you all on this bright pride day
Rainbow is everyone
No matter how much they protest

June 24, 2020

Rainbow is free to be
Rainbow is shade never made anybody less gay
Rainbow is being a human being
Rainbow is love who you may

June 24, 2020

One word is too simple to define
People have a complex mind
Nothing is simple as
Crossing a line
So defining what we have
Is more than a word, with one
Meaning
More than just heat = sun
You are not just an award to be won
Words are shapes cut out of light
You know I'm right

June 25, 2020

Death by a dozen cuts
Every place you touched
Burning
Tearing me apart
If the story is over
Why do I still have pen to paper
The ink bleeding like my body
You took so much of me
Stabbing me
Again and again
With the paper as useless as you
The pictures a constant reminder
One song reminds me of you

And another of my love
At least
I know he will never hurt me
He took the paper cuts
And wrapped them up
Kissing my heart
He is the angel that
Rose from the
Shredded paper
And helped me
Find the smile
I had lost
Because of you
He's my London boy
And guess what
You may live five minutes away
But I will always choose him
Over you
I fancy him
Not you
I love him and I never
Loved you
So quit trying to call

June 25, 2020

It's so excruciating to see you low
Just wanna lift you up and not let you go

June 26, 2020

Eighteen
Was a dream
I had an eight in my age
And I wrote my name on the page
So they rhymed and life was great
But now it is time to move on
I had a great time
Graduation
Invitation
To go great places
At the age of 18

July 4, 2020

Do you ever feel like
you are just drifting
further and further apart from someone?

It feels like a rushing river
rising higher and higher
drowning you until you can't hear anything.

Only the sounds of deafness
as water fills them deeply.

July 4, 2020

I stay up late to talk to you
Yet you seem to not respond much
Always better things to do
I waste my life staring at an empty screen
So much so I want to scream
You are fading
Just a dream
I don't want to complain
But it hurts my heart and my brain
I'm sorry

July 4, 2020

I feel like my birthday balloon
Every day I deflate just a little
Every day my mood crumbles just a little more
Every day I get closer
And closer to the ground
To the inevitable
Everything frustrating
Swaying in the wind
Bouncing back and forth
Twirling slowly
Downwards

July 5, 2020

The tears fall down
Puddle at my chin
It feels as though I'll never win
She yells at me for something stupid
Shows me that
My cousins matter, I fall flat
I cry so hard my heart constricts
I feel the pain
And as I predict
She doesn't care about me
She wakes me up
To find their things
I find nothing, she pulls my string
She doesn't even feed me
Starving
Falling on the floor
I try to leave, go out the door
And it is clear if I did
She wouldn't stop me

July 7, 2020

Feels like sitting in front of the stars
You scream to them
Begging them to talk
But
No matter how much you talk to them
They will never talk back
They will never cry out to you
Silent
Always
And with every scream my own throat
Starts to burn

July 8, 2020

Being without you is like falling down a waterfall
My heart jumping in my chest
As I free fall into what I know
Will be my death
I close my eyes
I feel the drops of water stain my skin
The wind rushing through my clothes and my hair
Slapping me on the face
But the fear of falling
Is nothing to me
Because the loneliness I felt
Before the fall
Was so much worse
Than inevitable death
Death is always at the end of the tunnel
But loneliness is not
So ending it
Is easier than feeling the pain
Of a million heartbreaks
Without you here

July 11, 2020

Two people at a crossroad
On the left
A field of flowers without stems
On the right
An empty home
Both calm, quiet, imperfect
Yet beautiful
One gets stung by a lonely bee
And the other hides in the dark
No one to see
But both alone
For eternity
Both people
Me

July 11, 2020

Who am I
Am I broken
Am I kind
Am I a lier
or a victim
Am I dumb
or truly smart
Who am I if not a lie
Who am I if not evil
Traits and labels are not just one box
They fit many people
I fear I am not just the good

July 12, 2020

She looks through the book
Of good and evil
Their type of thinking is medieval
They tried to say she wasn't allowed
To be the Pan that made her proud
They shouted and they did so scream
Hate seemed to be a common theme
So
Spread love and education
Not hate and misinformation

July 12, 2020

All the voices in my head
Pulsing through me like blood
Filling me with every breath
As my heart rate quickens
Fading with the time
The voices blind my eyes crimson
Screaming out across the line
Like chemicals burning my lungs
All my different anxieties
Becoming one

July 15, 2020

You take the knife
Smiling at me as you plunge it
Between my breasts
Blood stuck in me like a wine
In a corkscrew bottle
You laugh at me
As I stumble and fall
Not caring that the only reason
That I am injured
Is because of you

July 17, 2020

It makes me mad
And a little bit sad
When people don't talk to me
For hours you see
Even though I spend hours
Staring at Twitter like watching flowers
Grow
It hurts ya know
When I give my all
And no one gives a fuck about me

July 17, 2020

Leaves for self
But abandons a friend
Friend cries tears
Feeling broken, lonely, and then
Friend leaves for self
And the cycle begins again

There is no winning
When it comes to mental health

One friend lost
Her heart broken and blue
Another one dancing alone
To the blues
And here I stand crying
Tears in my eyes
I feel lonely
Dying inside

July 19, 2020

Deep breaths in.
Let the air fill your lungs
until you feel like a balloon.
Up and up
let it fill the room.
Then back out.
Deflate little by little.
There we go,
you'll be as fit as a fiddle.

July 19, 2020

I'm the woman you see
I won't leave you be
I'm the one who giggles with glee
Because you are the key
To my lock and I love you, sweet pea
I'm the woman you see, I won't leave you be
And one day I'll get down on one knee
Or we both will, probably
Cause we both know we love one another
I'll be by your side forever, baby
I'm the woman you see
I will never flee
As long as you promise me
You'll do the same

July 20, 2020

My hands wrap around your waist

        Our lips meet together for the first time

I let you give me a taste

        Not seeing you has gotta be a crime

This is one want I've not yet faced

        One mountain I've not yet climbed

I love you, saying less is a waste

        And so when we meet

I will kiss you with chaste

        And wrap my hands around your waist

July 21, 2020

How can I tell if I have depression?

All I ever do is repression and regression.
I never let myself feel the tension
Of overstressin' or give sadness the attention.

And did I mention

I usually hide the emotion
To help others, my intention,
I never show the full extension
Of what I feel inside.

So how can I tell I have depression,
If all I ever do is lock myself in
A permanent detention,
And trap my emotions in suspension,
Never fully showing the tension
I feel in my heart, soul, and mind?

How do I tell if I have depression?

You don't have that
My pretty little cat
Just take deep breaths
-L

July 21, 2020

I know I told you I didn't mind
That it was fine
But you must be blind
Because that was a lie
And that hurt
How you were curt
And you blurted
Out a single sentence
It really stung
And it rung through my head
Bouncing around and around again
And then
I cried
Dying inside
Because you weren't in the mood
To talk
You just walked
Right around the issue
So here I sit
A little bit pissed
Crying at the stupidity
That was you

July 25, 2020

I am an old cardigan
The color faded
And the material frayed
Sticking to your skin
Too stretched out
Too broken
Tossed on the floor
And crumpled under a bed
Will you put me on
And say I love you
Will you show me everything
Will you be mine
For a lifetime

July 25, 2020

What would happen if I changed the ending
If I was the one that was offending
& what you did was pending
And I was apprehending
My own heart
What if Wendy never went with Peter
What if Belle never loved the Beast
What if The Grinch never made it to the feast
What would we be

July 27, 2020

I was an old cardigan
color faded, material frayed
Stickingtoyourskin
Too   stretched   out
Too broken
Tossed on the floor
And crumpled under your bed

              You found the invisible----- string
                Glowing as blue as the tears
                  On my cracked face
                   And scarred skin
                   And it led me to you
                One single-------- thread
                  Tied {us} together

                           One in a million people
                             I could have found
                             When I desperately
                             Tried to find a friend
                              But I found you

You picked me up
Dusted off the dirt
Threw me in the wash
Showed me my color
Put me on
And told me I looked beautiful

You were the one
That kissed it better
The one that took this old cardigan
And showed it the beauty
It always had been

You put me on
And said I love you
You put me on and
Showed me everything
You didn't need anything bright
You didn't need anything perfect
All you wanted was me

The American
And her London Boy
And now I see
That we are both an old cardigan
And I love you just the same

July 29, 2020

I find lady luck & ask her my fortune
As she hides behind silver locks
Curled with time
She tells me I have none
For although my day was filled with sweets
My night is not sugar
I bid her goodnight
As tears blanket my face
Keeping me warm
From the stinging chill
of loneliness

July 29, 2020

It is always the same
When I am not busy
No one calls my name
It makes me dizzy
This boring game
Getting me into a tizzy
This is not why I came
Back to this app, ya see
I needed a distraction
Especially tonight
But I see that is not going to happen
My tears not a pleasant sight

August 2, 2020

I'm sick and tired of waiting for you
It's like waiting for a flower to bloom
On top of the ever glowing moon
I crave the respect I am due
Yet here I am nine in the afternoon
Stuck still waiting for you

August 2, 2020

You are the poison that seeps into my veins
Turning blue dark black as it melts into my blood
Your mouth speaks one way
Yet your feet move away from you
You are the epitome of hate
Once invisible to me
Now clearly seen
And so I fade away from you
Do not hope to see my wedding
Do not hope to hold my child
You are dead to me
Because like a ghost
You can not see the future

August 5, 2020

My mouth speaks yet nothing comes out
Frantically yelling without sound
As my body shakes with emotion
You had stabbed me in the back
Draining my blood from me
Like water from a tap
                    Liar

                    You wrote my consent in blood
                    Conned

                    You told them it was someone else
                    Hurt

                    You broke me when I was already dying

My mouth speaks yet nothing comes out
Frantically yelling without sound
From you pulling my vocal cords out of my heart
As my body frantically shakes with emotion
You had taken my inspiration from me
Stabbing me in the back
Without remorse or questions asked
Draining the thing keeping me alive
Like water from a tap

August 6, 2020

Two hearts reflected back at me
Through the smudged mirror
Of my past life
Pink turning red
As I learn to love again
Words blurred in my eyes
That can no longer see
From tears that show me
That you
Have helped me to be
Better
Loved
Forever

August 8, 2020

Don't have anything to do
Don't have anywhere to go
I have so many feelings
I just wish to go home
Used to be stuck like glue
Now I feel so low
You were my healing
And now I'm alone

August 8, 2020

I never understood trends
And I don't think I ever will
They don't make any sense
And I don't like the thrill
The only trend I've ever partaken in is "tea to spill"
Don't get me wrong. Like what you want, it's chill
But I don't understand trends
And I don't think I ever will

August 11, 2020

The taste of salt mixes with the water
My dehydrated tongue needs most
Falling to replenish my lips
I wish you were here to hold me close
Wrapping arms around me
Protective box
But distance spreads us apart
I wish your words were here
Wrapping warmth around me
But you aren't

August 14, 2020

Fingers fall against worn letters
Loose lips forming words
With both fingers and tongue
Of course when I have no one to talk to
Is when it hits the hardest
The need to
The want to
The craving
Good Doctor says to talk more
But when there is no one to talk to
Who do I talk to?
If fingers fall then who are they falling for?
If letters wear away, who are they going to?
If I have no one to talk to
How do I let out
The need to?
The want to?
The crave to?
When I need you
Want you
Crave you
How do I let it out?
You have your own life
I am not your wife
This is not your strife
I could cut the tension with a knife
And in my imagination, it would still be there

I cannot bear
For you to see me like this
But I need you to see
That me
When I need you now
You aren't here
And I know you didn't make a vow
I know this isn't a big deal
Or a final bow
I'm not in immediate danger
But you are acting like a stranger
And I need to let this out
How do I let out
The need to?
The want to?
The crave to?
When I need you
Want you
Crave you
I see now that even surrounded by people
I am hidden
Because no one talks to me
I need you, I want you, I crave you
But you never understand what I plead for
I need you to be there
I want you to talk
I crave to communicate
And it is never worth the wait
Not when I never get it

August 15, 2020

Killer hornets came to call
When a virus was already leading to our downfall
Then came a man being killed
An injustice
It showed that cops never were skilled
They have to rebuild
Defunded
Then the country was split
Between Black lives matter and those that don't
wanna admit
They are racist
Saying he died because of noncompliance
Not because the cop's reliance
On excess force and ignorance
On top of all that
Came an orange ape man
And his white rich people klan
Stopping the mail and the election
Wearing no masks and not using protection
All because they are idiots and all types of hideous
Because "it is what it is"
When people are dying
But showers and mail are worth crying
And they try and say he isn't lying
But he's stated more falsehoods
Then he's had an orgasm
And that's not even sarcasm

More people have shown their true selves
Then libraries have shelves
And it really goes to show who is hateful and dumb
And where they come from
Cause saying that what we experience is fake
Or that he deserved to break
Cause his black life didn't matter
And that mail in votes are just clatter
And gonna cause a catastrophe
Is nothing more than an anastrophe
Spoken by a madman
We live in a world
Falling to pieces
As ignorance increases
Coming out of the shadows
All of the worst fears
Are coming clear
And it would appear
The year
Keeps
Getting
Worse

August 15, 2020

I wish, I wish, I wish to dye my hair myself
But the dye I use is from the shelf
And no one trusts me to do it right
I wish, I wish, I wish to practice makeup now
But that would waste more than I would allow
So I leave it brand new until school
I wish, I wish, I wish to bake
But my grandparents are not awake
When it comes to being safe
I wish, I wish, I wish I could see my best friend
But she is not safe so we both comprehend
That we have to stay apart
I wish, I wish, I wish to visit a library
But I am way too wary
To go anywhere right now
There are so many things I wish I could do
And I know that I can't so it makes me feel blue
I wish I could take the happiness I was due
But I actually think things through
And it would not be fair to be unsafe cause I knew
That being safe is being true
To who I am and helping you
I may be suffering mentally which is new
But since it means saving lives I do it two
Times over, every time, to save the few
I may have hurt if it blew
Through me

I want you to see
That inevitably
My brain does wish to be
Anywhere else and flying free
So I offer up my glee
Confused and laying here uncomfortably
Wishing to be
Anywhere but laying in bed
Feeling dead
Confused in the head
For you

August 18, 2020

I am stressed
Maybe depressed
Who knows
But my phone
Is broken
I dropped a book
On my foot
I stepped on a wet mat
And when I sat
I fell off the bed
Why is today so bad
But yesterday I was glad
I really don't know what to do
I finally see through
Myself
I need a break
Not something fake
I need to regress
To hide all the awful feelings inside
My mind
Breaking apart
I'm sorry I am not
Giving you my heart
It all hurts
Pushing in like invisible walls
Claustrophobic
Trying not to scream

Heavy start
Chaotic mind
Swirling deeper
I hear them say

"Could you ever really keep her"

"She is too up and down"

"Always smile or frown"

"She acts like a clown"

"She isn't even pretty"

I know I freak out at the smallest of things
And I know I'm not an angel with wings
I come with many strings
Attached

August 25, 2020

The worry and panic fills my head
I don't think anyone will understand
My mind swirling deep and dark
You never ever miss the mark
My brain tells me you are dead
Because I don't know what is in your head
It really hurts to have you gone
Maybe you are sleeping until a new dawn
The fear and anxiety creeps up on me
I've ignored it all day you see
I needed you when you were missing
But I had a pen so I started listing
Things that made me happy
Most of them were sappy
And now I am worried once more
And so I have to let my dreams soar
Because if I keep
Thinking I will explode
It really is such a load
I really need you
To know
You are safe
You are okay
You are not hurt
Because all this thinking

I can't anymore

August 26, 2020

A shadow surrounds me
Caving in
Grabbing my heart
Like chains
And pulling tight
Constricting
The light fading
Ghost awakening
Why did it hurt
When no one
Hurt me

August 27, 2020

Life is everything at once
Thoughts melding together with
Words and memories
Ideas turning shapes against the
Overwhelming perspective of billions
In all of my life, I wished for you
A little girl whose dream was love

Regret is human
Making mistakes and reversing
Turning back time to apologize
For ideas, for words, for actions
Yet moving forward to more errors

In all my life I never will regret you
A dream fulfilled by your love

Success is trying to be seen
Being as perfect as perfect can be
Just shouting out me, me, me
And throwing money out in glee
After all the hard work, all of the pleas
But I'd give up trying for success
Because you are all I need

Children are the future
The superheroes of the world
Taught love and shown how to heal
To change the world that makes us feel
Like there is no future worth saving
In all my life I have always wanted children
A dream we can make reality together

Happiness is easy to find and hard to keep
More than just a smile and a little leap
Of joy deep within our hearts
It fades faster than time yet it is easier
Than a rhyme to find
In all my life I've never stayed happy
A dream I thought I wouldn't achieve …
But you gave me it
Faith is believing in things
You may never understand

Holding strong to ideals and thoughts ingrained
In a mind twisted and chained
A princess trained
To think a little faith, trust, and pixie dust
Will guide the way
But I would give up faith in the unknown
Because you are all I need

Work is making money and having fun
An equal balance between stability and happiness
Not needing hobbies, for work is the best hobby
Living days with smiles on faces
And income in cases, for the rest of our days
In all my life I have always wanted both
A dream you have helped me see

Peace is unachievable, nothing but a dream
Hate and pride blinding all humanity
From painting with the colors of the wind
Not able to stand hand in hand
Because division is the world
In all my life I have thought peace was the answer
But you showed me a different perspective

Religion is storytelling that divides the earth
Everyone trying to claim how we could be rebirthed
People judging stranger's worth
And never letting anyone express mirth
Always stuck in the same old berth

But I would give up arguing with ignorant assholes
Because your time is worth more than theirs

Love is a strong tie to others, linked by souls
A heart tied to another heart
And a mind understood by another mind
Like a neverending ribbon
You are mine
You are my life, my success, my happiness,
My faith, my peace, my religion
My love

August 30, 2020

My heart breaks as my mind lingers
Scars on my fingers
From pressing nails into skin
I don't think I'll ever win
I had hoped to spend the day
Talking but it turned out they
Didn't feel the same way
And so now I say
Nothing at all
Letting the tears fall
Broken and upset
Today was the last day
I could message as long as I may
Because tomorrow school starts
And my education is where my heart
Will lay when school does commence
And so I was going to talk an immense
Amount today
But that is not what they say
And not the way
It went down today
No one to play
And so I say
Nothing at all
Letting the tears fall
Broken and upset

Fall

September 1, 2020

She holds my cheeks trying
To stop the tears that overflow
Yet all she manages to do is
Build them up against my eyes
Burning
Hurting
Pain blurred by my own saltwater
"Is it even worth it?" I whisper
An unspoken question meant for the heavens
She smiled sadly at me
"Why are you asking me?
I'm just a ghost of a memory gone by."
She spoke softly
Her voice like the twinkling of bells
Sweet cotton candy to my ears
Turning sour in my head
I want to ask
Why is it that
I need to talk yet all I hear is silence
The therapist said communication
Is key
Yet all I see are locks
Because no one lets me in
Either barred from talking
Or barring themselves from talking
I want to ask
Why is it that

I need structure in my daily life
To do things that make me happy
Yet there is never time to
Because either they are busy
Or I am
The therapist said I should continue this
But how can I when my game for two
Only ever sees me
I want to ask
Why is it that
I need friends
Yet I'm left wondering why I am the only one
Ever putting in the work
I want to ask
Why is it that I have these issues with
My mind
Is it the pain from being alone for so long
Is it the pain from always being let down
Is it the pain from being pushed away
I don't know
But I am sick of trying
I am sick of being let down
I am told to communicate
I am told to do this because it gives structure
It gives me joy
It brings me closer to my friends
But ... as I lay here crying
Just like almost every night
I can't help but wonder

Were my friends nothing more than an illusion?
She brings me into her arms
And wipes away the tears
"At least you have me."
"Yes."
I whisper
"But you are nothing more than a past
version of myself that I talk to and wonder
what could have been ... if I had just never
started this in the first place."
I hug myself
My own arms wrapped around my waist
As I wipe away my own tears
For another time that night.
Tonight.

September 1, 2020

I disagree.
Psychology taught me differently.
It is not a symptom.
And it can occur with more than just depression.
Not to mention.
It is a result of something.
That is why we are taught about it
as a separate thing.
Not a symptom.

September 4, 2020

You're gonna miss me when I'm gone
Fading away
Morning to dawn
Every day

You're gonna miss me by my hair
The hair you loved
And you were well aware
You said I was beloved
But I clearly was not

You're gonna miss me everywhere, oh
You're gonna miss me when I'm gone

You're gonna miss me when I'm gone
Never responding
In any way
No more bonding
Every day

You're gonna miss me by my walk
You never got to see
The pure shock
Of never being with me

You're gonna miss me by my talk, oh
You're gonna miss me when I'm gone

September 5, 2020

Never fear me when I'm loud.
Fear me when I say nothing at all.
It is often those that stay quiet
That have the most to say.
Not with words, but with what they aren't saying.

September 11, 2020

The earth beneath me shook violently
Invisible dirt tearing the grass apart and splitting
Our world in two
I stayed standing
But I could tell you were tumbling
Torn through the middle
And crashing in on yourself
Holding yourself
As you rocked back and forth
I know, you know, she knew, he knew, we know
You weren't planning for forever
We weren't meant for each other
Weren't meant to last
And it's fine
But if the world was ending
You'd come home, right?
You'd want to be here

Want to be with me and my family
If the world was ending I would still act
As I am now
Standing tall
Shocked as the ground was torn apart
And I watched with no thoughts in my mind
And no words leaving my lips

Would you bring her with you
And say hello
To those you left behind?
Lost friend
Did you see the chaos and decide
We would be better off without you?
Because here I stand
In an Earthquake
My world shook to the core
With my heart ripped from my chest
I know, you know, she knew, he knew, we know
You weren't planning for forever
We weren't meant for each other
Weren't meant to last
And it's fine
But if the world was ending
You'd come home, right?

September 11, 2020

Goodnight, love
Spoken with a kind whisper
Understanding in her aura
And no pain in her soul
Laying down a leaf and starting
A new chapter
Another beginning
Moving forward to see the world
Again

Goodnight, darling
Spoken with a surprised whisper
Shock in her aura
And confusion in her soul
Planting a tree and starting
A new series
Another beginning
Moving forward to see the world
Once more

Goodnight, love
Goodnight, pure dove
Goodnight, one up above

Goodnight, darling
Goodnight, starling
Goodnight, starring friend

Goodnight, moon
Goodnight, June
Goodnight
Way too soon

September 12, 2020

Once upon a time
We were in the same constellation
But you flew so far away
I was circumpolar
Never setting
And you were
A supernova
Dead
Spread to the clouds
And reborn from your ashes
Phoenix rising
We were too far away to touch
Too far away
I asked you to orbit me
But you couldn't even do
The bare minimum
For me

September 12, 2020

I hate always being stabbed by the people
Who are supposed to help me heal
They trade bandages for weapons
And kindness for selfishness
Taking their knives
Stabbing me in the back
And while I am already down
Shooting me with a gun
Designed by their own hands
They spread red to my lips
And as I taste the sourness of my own blood
They leave me in the dust
Even as I beg them
To hold my dying hand

September 12, 2020

I'm the queen of broken hearts
Broken in a thousand shards
Scars sewing together every part
Of my breaking body
I am a puzzle
Of blood and skin and bones
All alone
And out of tone
Stitched together like a modern Frankenstein
Every piece of my crown another thorn
Tearing into my skin
Every day
A piece of me fading
Into a daydream
I am a story
Stuck in my mind
Because real life has broken me
They break me apart
Lover
Friend
Enemy
To make me a queen

September 13, 2020

My beautiful heart
When you are blue
I am too
Hanging my head
And crying tears
I never knew I had

My truest friend
When you need a friend
I offer my ear once again
I want you to talk
Not push you away
To hide your head

My kind lover
I miss you
You miss me too
But I want you to be happy
And I know it is sappy
But sometimes I need to
Close my eyes
To see a smile on your face

September 19, 2020

Who am I if not a writer
You smear my lips in watered down paint
And expect me not to feel my heart
Constricting in a box
Made of licorice and twine
You whine
Complaining about your own miseries
Yet don't think twice about the prison
I have to let my creativity live in
Who are you if not broken
Lashing out not caring who broke in
To tear down the poster of my mind
You are supposed to raise me up
Not fill my cup
With poison
Who are we if not together

September 19, 2020

My lips are bleeding
Natural lipstick shimmering in the sunlight
Staining my lips a permanent red
I take my pen and stab them
Where they hurt me most
The blood filling the pen sprouting from them
Caverns of broken skin
Ripped like paper
Pulled apart to reveal the mess of the human body
My victims laying submissively beneath me
Their voices frozen in time
Like they had done to me
As I walk calmly away from the scene

I write with crimson ink
Nothing good enough for me
The pain too great to use anything else
You tell me I'll be alright in the morning
That my lips will never have to bleed again
Yet you never told me they would be stained
And so I will slice you all open, I will reign
Endlessly taking the veins
Of the predators that had once slain
The precious princess locked in the tower
Locked away in my cage of innocence

I wake up every morning

With a pen waiting to be filled
And so I will continue to wake up
And attach them to my bed
Filling my blood into tiny plastic bottles
Until one day they die, body squeezed of blood
As I had when they had carved my name
Into their bedpost
No more juice in my heart
No more water in my body

And then I will write
The words of crimson color
Staining the wooden floors
You tell me I'll be okay
But I never was from the start
I'm the queen of broken hearts
Hurt
Killed
And now reborn
Stained me
Strained me
Sprained me
So pain plea
Begging me
To release you

September 20, 2020

When the tables are turned
The game is no longer fun anymore
A target carved deep into my back
And the smell of dying flesh
Wrapped around me

When the tables are turned
Loneliness sinks in
Marked with x's with a knife
And the smell of harassment
Wrapped around my brain

When the tables are turned
The day darkens further
Sticking a white flag through my heart
And the smell of salty tears
Wafting off my cheeks

When the tables turn
My mind starts turning with it

September 21, 2020

The truth is I don't know
I don't know if I can handle
Moving my shoes across the water
Your tears are too many for me to handle
The rain falling from your eyes filling
The material, soaking in
And making me sink quicker
I don't know if I can do it
I don't know if my mind can handle the trip
I don't even know if the warmth
I feel is fake or fiction
An illusion of a trapped mind
I don't know if it will last
Because I don't know if I can let it
I want rainbows
Not a constant pool of water
Because then I will never get anywhere

October 4, 2020

Scoop up my eyes for I have no need for them
Scoop up my head for it has gone now
Scoop up my heart for it --

Oh wait, my heart still constricts
Reminded of a blurry past

Never wanted

Yet I always

Try again

October 17, 2020

Life lived in sadness is not reality
We must experience both happiness and sadness
We must think both with the head and the heart

To truly live

Humans can be happy just as they can be sad
It is stupid to say we are always sad even when we
are happy
For that is false

October 26, 2020

Heated tears cascade down my face
I feel like such a disgrace
Words, my trade
Have now betrayed me
Slitting my skin
Letting blood soak in
Frustration squeezing my heart
Before I even start
20 could not be handled
Yet 57 ... oh the scandal
Hurts my broken heart

November 1, 2020

I am a sinsemilla
You must take all the other males
Away from me
To keep me
I am dangerous by myself
Used, abused
A beautiful piece of nature
Seen as nothing more than poison
I am a sinsemilla
I hurt others because they hurt me
For those who don't know me
I am invisible

November 1, 2020

My eyes roam over paper
Heavy despite ten plus one hour
Dreaming, no nightmares so sour

Asleep overnight

My head not able to concentrate on the words
Dizzy like an airsick bird
Once in a million lifetimes

I cannot focus

My stomach tells me no food
My love tells me to do
What I need to

But it all makes me so blue
Because I have work to do
And so I let my mind wander over paper
As empty as water vapor
Drowned

November 9, 2020

Silhouette fades to grey
Looking in the mirror
Distorted features opaque
Out of the way
As she sits atop a marbled rock
In the middle of the lake
Alone

She takes a bottle of crystallized glass
Scooping tears of the waterfall of pain
As clouds above fade to grey
Sealing the top
With a cork of her own saltwater
Waiting on the wind
A lone girl

Girl all alone
A lone girl all alone
Known as alone
No more than alone
Forever

November 9, 2020

Find me between nowhereland
Where friends fall fast
And time has twisted dry like sand
Where the present is the past
And friends never last

Find me between Falsehoodtown
Where they promise you forever
And lips are twisted into a permanent frown
Where conversations sever
Oh we thought we were so clever

Find me between forest and sea
Where everything isn't what it ought to be
And nothing is what you want to see
Where there is just "I" and never a "we"
Find me in the in-between

November 16, 2020

My body is slowly breaking apart
The loneliness feels like a dart in the heart
Bones crushed down by a blanket made of weight
Creates agony oh I truly hate
To feel like I am slowly deteriorating

Leg stands straight like a cast
Joy cannot ever last
Because if I bend I break

My heart cries out for someone to talk to
My head cries out in pain, happy days few

Give me attention
Fake your affection
Just give me something, please
Listen to my pleas

Before I explode

November 17, 2020

I feel stuck in this weird in between
Nothing to do and no one to see
Please oh please set me free
I don't wanna be stuck in this weird in between

November 25, 2020

My eyes are heavy
My bed mingling with seven to ten
Caressing skin and pillow to head
You see sun and moon
Yet your eyes are not weighted down
I see you and I have to frown
For I want to lay down your tired crown
But all you say is not yet

Not yet
Almost
Maybe
No

And through it all, I have to groan
Because it worries me
The constant anxiety
Of what could happen to you
Because of what you do

Not yet
Almost
Maybe
No

Why must you stoop so low
And hurt yourself I must know

Because it isn't fair to yourself
...
...
Or me

November 25, 2020

You made me cry today
The tears spread down my cheeks
A veil of a different kind
I told you I would be your bride
But this was not what I meant

I do not marry anxiety
I divorce it

I do not birth my fear
I reverse it

I do not kiss my tears
I converse it

You made me cry today
Parting my veil of a different kind
Usually, I do not mind

But you crushed my soul today

Winter

December 13, 2020

Today is the day where blue fades from worn eyes
And dances across the pages of my memory
Painting nothing but absolute glee
For my wide smile to see
The artist in me claims that
Blue never was a sad color
Even though the others tear my dreams in two
Now I rise and stand
Taller
Happier
Brighter
As the blue glimmers across my nails
All around the land
"Today is the day," I say
The day to be happy
To be overjoyed
And to take the label of blue
And apply it to you

Happiness in a bottle

December 14, 2020

Waterfall child born from the rain
Twists and tumbles out of her broken bubble
She bobs on the rushing waves
Rocks pelting her skin and sticks digging
Cutting into her bones
Red mixing with blue
To make a pink lemonade
Sour in her open mouth
That was in and out of the river
Trying to scream for someone to save her
From the ever moving night
Yet not even the flies try to save her breaking bones
The stars laugh as the fall grows near
Shimmering in a taunt that glistened in her eyes
Soaked by unidentifiable water
Salt rubs into her wounds
Like sandpaper on bare eyes
The noise of the rush blinding her ears
Like the rush of the blood leaving her veins
Three inches, Two inches
And then down she falls
Freely she flies
Until the bone-cracking belly flop
Where everything stops
The ultimate demise

Like a single tear against pavement

December 16, 2020

Woman of the water
Sees the world for what it is
Birthed from pain and anger
Bubbling in the pit of her frozen heart
Boneless and bloodless as she sinks ever further
Into the deep dark depths of the dim plunge pool

There is no noise
Because her breath has been taken
There is no temperature
For her body has been ripped
Like a piece of paper in a child's hands

There is no time
For her time is gone

Woman of the water
Sees the world for what it is

Dead
Silent

For she is nothing but a tear

On the pavement

December 17, 2020

She crawls out of the deep dark depths
Of the perfect plunge pool
Dragging nails into the ground
As she slithered to the surface
Her freeze-dried sticks of hair sticking up
A thorny crown of a different kind
As her eyes take in her surroundings
Broken bones mixing with snow
Adding solid to liquid
As her breath mixes with the wind
Icicles binding her grey skin closed
Leaking into her skin
And pouring pain into her vein
Blood of lilac-blue
Not knowing what to do
As the heavens leak upon her
A dress of white, And diamond pearls
As she says "I do" to a groom
That takes everything from her and gives
Her nothing in return
Laying in her shallow grave
Two feet deep in the eternal winter

Just a teardrop
On the pavement
Twisted, Turned
And dead on impact

December 26, 2020

Standing on the edge overlooking the
Pitch black dark of night
Fading through the emptiness
And waiting for something
Anything at all
Stuck in a never ending fall
In a world of glass emotions
I shatter

Too weak to stand tall
But too strong to sink through
To where the beginning meets the end
Twisting, turning, around the dimly lit bend
Standing on the edge overlooking the
Pitch black dark of night
Heartbreak my only name because
I shatter

I fall, break, and become a million pieces
As the water consumes my face
Locking me in a helmet of aqua blue
That no sound can get through
Fading through the emptiness
And waiting for something, anything at all
I shatter like the tear I have become
Broken for the same reason I was born
Human Emotion

December 27, 2020

I put my locket in your hands
But you dropped it

You took the bulb not lit
Hiding light until it split

You jammed the key in the lock
And mocked me
Breaking the steel heart laying like a sin

You dug the chain into my neck
Until it burned me
Tattooing the heartbreak on my skin

You carved a smile into my cheek
And a frown into my hand
Telling me to forgive again
Because you hurt me once more

Tick tock
Goes my clock
Yet the pain lasts forevermore

December 29, 2020

You promised me a diamond ring
Yet fine sand falls from your cracked
And bleeding fingers
Burying me in an hourglass of your own design
I try to sink through to the other side
To save myself
More time

Tick, tick, tick, tock
Yet the clock has me trapped

The sand fills my lungs turning the red sea
Into a dark desert
Hidden away in my body
Mummify me
Deep in the ground

Tick, tick, tick, tock
Yet the clock never stops

Promise me life
Yet death is what I have become
Glassy eyes staring frozen at the wall
Waiting for a fall
That would never come

Tick, tick, tick, tock

In the clock I stay locked

Waiting for a better day
Where we don't rise just to fall
With a better place to lay

January 5, 2021

My hands grab the jagged rock
Piercing my skin as blood pours
From empty wounds, Each step tearing my body
Like tape wrongly adhered to a paper
Ripped more than just what it was from the page
I get to the top, looking down at the world below
My blood wrapping around my arms like sleeves
Dripping down from my ruby fingers
I was nothing until compressed
Turning into a glimmering pearl
You push me, making me fall deeper
Cry more, until I am submerged in saltwater
Stuck beneath the waves
Push
Trap me in your pain in the silence of the water
Rebirth
Made from the water
Now brand new
All from the painful moments
Past and present, Perfect pearl

January 10, 2021

Will you love me even if skin once porcelain
Was cracked clay dried out by time?

Will you love me even if snow falls
From locks of false gold?

Will you love me even if every line
No longer rhymes?

Will you love me even if my mind
Is already sold?

Will you love me if there is hair
Everywhere, because I like locks long?

Will you love me for all imperfections
In my complexion
And no direction
In my life

Strife my only mindset?

Will you love me with all your affection
Despite all my objections
About my lack of perfection
Even though your selection
Was for our connection, love?

January 13, 2021

The sweater that promised to keep her warm
When she was young
Filled with holes from the swarm
Poking, prodding, and pulling free

Shivering, she walks
Trying to find a place to lay
Her teeth chattering, she tried to talk
Cold snaking, slithering, and slipping free

She finds no home or safe space
In the dark black hole of the earth
So she lays her head on torn pant lace
Turning, twisting, and twirling free

She sleeps till the morning
Weary eyes opening wide
The sky her only warning
Snow falling, fainting, flittering free

Burry me
In the cold
Until I can no longer see
And I am free to be
Me

January 13, 2021

Bored out of my mind
I can't find anything to do
It is a signature with nothing to sign
It is talking but nothing kind
It is a book without a bind
It is paper with no line
Able to hear but blind
Nothing to unwind
Resigned to remind mankind
I am confined to loneliness

January 14, 2021

Half-past and not working fast
Just sitting here doing nothing
Here I am again but then
I disappear far away from there
Nowhereland where the waves crash
Is where I begin my journey with a splash
Into the Everlast waterfall
I cannot see you
All alone one minus two
Missing myself and you again
Into the Nowhereland

January 14, 2021

Never buy me a rose
Because flowers are a reminder
That life never lasts
Never looking as they did in the past

Sweet perfume goes sour
After just a few hours
And petals once fine
Brittle and dry, no longer mine

But the smell is sweet and kind
So now that you mention it maybe I don't mind
To be treated like royalty
Buy me a rose

Or two ... or three
Show me
We are meant to be

Be romantic and gentle and sweet
And when we meet
The flowers will remind me
We are meant to be

Even if everything withers and dies
Roses can be wise
And the ultimate prize

To show romantic love

Never buy me a rose for something big and grand
It is the little things that make me understand

So surprise me and take my hand
Offer me a rose when I don't expect
And take a day and make it less bland

With the roses of the land

January 15, 2021

She laid in a patch of red and orange and brown
Staring at the sky like an old friend
Seeing where she had begun from where she was
She had danced like the bed of leaves
That surrounded her
Flitter, flutter, fly

Aren't they so pretty when they fall?

A few tears dripping down her cheeks
Her lips turned up in a permanent smile
She felt at peace
The world turning beneath her burning body
As leaves continued to paint her fallen form
All leaves die alone in the end

Leaves die together, not alone.
That's why they all lay on the ground together.
Beautiful even when not green,
Even though harsh winters can be mean,
Leaves come together and make a team,
to fill people with such glee,
Giving a sense of peace,
Something we all need.

It's not always clear what they mean,
But when you think about it ...
They're all pleasant like a dream.
Whether during or after a storm
Or when the rain starts to pour,
They change a little bit to maintain their form.
Providing smiles, making life worthwhile,
Just like everyone in our lives.

-L

January 16, 2021

Who are we to judge ourselves?
We aren't plastic dolls sitting on shelves

Society is comprised of values
Where everyone must dress
But no one can impress
Themselves

Little girl grows up with sags in her skin
And so many stretch marks
She feels like she'll never win
Her bumps from broken DNA
Makes her feel like clothing that's frayed
Broken and tossed away

She sits in her bed, poking her pudgy belly
Thinking "Well I don't look like the girls on tele."
She doesn't realize that one day
Her belly will be where life goes to lay
A beautiful part of her body
The body she thought was shoddy
And her sags will get saggier
And her stretchmarks will stretch wider
From holding a baby deep inside her
That she and her partner had created
In a body that once upon a time she had hated

So while she sits in her room
Poking at an empty womb
Hurting her self esteem
Being mean
To herself

Maybe she should think
Think long and hard
We all are a little bit scarred

Trying to be thinner
Because apparently, that is a winner
In our doomed society

Weight is compression from gravity
But society feeds us lies until we feel like cavities
Filling up space like waste
Poking at our flaw-filled face
Until there is so much hate in our hearts
We don't even see the beauty in our own parts

We take little girls all across the world
All the they, ze, zirs, and others
We take all the boys
And we treat everyone like toys
Teaching no self-love to one another

January 17, 2021

I feel dead
No, it's just my head
From the pain
That reigns from strain
Broken eyes peer through glass windows
Shattered and torn
Breaking down Iris' that are already worn
From a twisted pain above my nose

January 18, 2021

I breathe in
Staring at white
As the mirror of what could be
Stares back at me
My mind is cleared
Cleaned
No cache left
And the data restored
To what had been
Before it fell apart
But now I am lost
Missing
Who am I
And who will I become

January 19, 2021

A castle built of tar and mud
Sways in the breeze
Sinking slowly into the water
That sunk against the side
Unstable sand filling the castle
Until only a puddle of tar remains
She slips on the mud
Hands waving in the air
As she tries to fly away
Stuck to the weight
Of the world
Tar stuck between her fingers
She thought she would be free
From the Karama
Free to live her way
But everyone saw
That her castle would fall
Before she even built it
Yet she cares little for their words
Because she knows
History is written by the heroes
And in her eyes, she is the hero
I know better
And so I will write the truth
Of the unstable sand in the unstable land
Of the mind of a villain

January 19, 2021

Karma whispers sweetly in my ear
In a purr and a roll of her tongue
An ever-present smirk
Resting on her delicate poison lips
As she wraps her arms around me
In a false hug
She tells me the deed is done
The next chapter published for all to read
To see the villain's heart deep beneath

She tells me that I was right
Painting confidence into my weak bones
Until only the vision of logic remains
In a brain of a delicate design

It breaks my heart
Cracking, ripping, shattering apart
Puncturing my skin until scars remain
And bruising the blank canvas of my chest
Disintegrating into dust
I did not want to be right
Heartless

Karma kisses my cheek like an old friend
Cursing all that hurt me
And loving me until the end of days

January 24, 2021

It's like cheating while running a race

      But then for the final lap, following the rules

It's like a disobedient dog

      Laying down the hundredth time you ask him to

It's like calling the new girl the right name

         On her last day of work

It's like not going to school

        On the last day before summer break

It's like covering your nose

         On your fourth sneeze

It's obvious to everyone but you
But it is useless and worthless too
To sit around being safe
When it's the last day you knew
Nothing at all

January 25, 2021

One splash can create a tidal wave
A single drop of water pouring from wounds
Soaking the cloth with red

The queen curls up into a ball
Wishing she was nothing at all
Just to rescue the pain
From becoming pouring rain

One splash can create a tidal wave
They all say
That one little tear
Can do nothing we'd fear
But the truth of the matter is that
It is as sickly as a plaque of half dead rats
Pouring from our eyes

The queen denies
That the pain has fallen
Too ashamed to rise and stand tall
Too afraid she'll continue to fall

Because her pain created a tidal wave
That ruined the whole city

January 25, 2021

She lays on the pavement
Too afraid to get up
Her bones snapped like a crayon
And her blood missing from her veins
Boiled away a long time ago

She curses the people of Earth
Broken and alone as she weeps into the cracks
Of the abandoned sidewalk
Creating salt and filling the mud with nutrients

Pale grey leaks into her form
Decayed and weary from her travels
Forgotten to all
Woman of the water becoming nothing more
Than sealant for a silly sidewalk
In the Southside of the city

Once a queen born from the clouds
And shaped by the waterfall
Now falling ever further down
Invisible pain
As storm clouds rain down on her

No more pleasure, gaining nothing
Broken Beauty turned into a Beast
For selflessness sake

January 28, 2021

The silence we feel
In the moments between the rush
In the moments between what was
In the moments before the storm
Must be what the moon feels
When the sky goes dark
And we go dark
As we close the blinds
Of our eyes
For the final time
In the day
Looking down on us as the quiet
Settles in
For the entire time
The moon is high
Awake and ready to play
The moon lives in silence
Never seeing the busy time the
Sun surely sees
But the moon does not envy the sun
Because sometimes
Silence is surprising
Because it calms our hearts
And makes our souls sour
The pleasure of a paused moment

February 2, 2021

A bird doesn't miss the sky
Until it can no longer fly
Its wings scared and broken
From hours of wear
Staring up at the sky
More sadness than it can bear

A fish doesn't miss the sea
Until it can no longer swim by
Its fins gasping for the tight embrace
Of the silk blue water
Dreary scales
Oh what a slaughter

We don't realize what we have until it is gone
We sit there and wonder all day long
Blind to the world
Selfish, for we only see
What we have and what we can be
And not what they are
So far
Shining Stars
Hidden from us all

A human doesn't miss their dreams
Until they clearly see
What we all had all along

February 4, 2021

I take the crystal bottle
Shimmering in the summer sun
And tip two drops of lavender
Past my chapped lips
Rough like sandpaper never worn down
Tossed aside in a cabinet and hidden from view
The liquid slides down my throat like a breath
And sinks into the pit of my stomach
A constant companion connected to me
Coupled in compassion and care

My eyes turn like a mood ring
Never staying the same as they once were
As the liquid settles deep within me
A magic of a different kind
Spellbound by beauty and brilliance
A brain as perfect as a body
Two souls become one
Time flies by like a clock on a string
Hypnotizing the world I see
Seven months slip by
And not even I
Recognize the person I have become

I rip the page from the crystal bottle
Sitting on the shelf now as empty as I once was
They called it everlast

For it stuck forever in the heart
Like a pin in a cushion
Doing the job it was meant to have
To satisfy self and help heal others

It is not lasting when
One lacks the understanding
To master the magic within

I take the bottle and look at my reflection
Multiplied by thousands and mirroring who I am
My violet eyes glowing
And my pink cheeks gleaming
As I whisper words of wonder
To unlock the magic within

You are my everlast

And love is the key

So thank you for loving me

February 7, 2021

She stares out at the city of crystal and snow
Watching the world get sucked into a whirlwind
As the prayers of the Praisers fell upon deaf ears
She had told her people to run
To find faith far away
And keep fear in the mind's eye as a motivator

But instead of running
They had thrown snow on the flame

She had explained that if you play hot potato
You are bound to get burned
But they hadn't cared
Getting their warmth from
The disease of a million hands
And the mouths of all the land

Their teeth glittering gold but their breath formed
From the carcasses of rats still oozing black blood

The people hugged Ignorance and befriended Hate
Locking arm in arm with the fate of death

She sighed and took a single breath
Walking to her room and locking the door
Waiting to die from the cold and invisible death
The people of her kingdom had caused

February 11, 2021

She felt the world twisting around her as she fell

                              Staring up at the sky

            As the circle of light shrunk ever smaller
                        Her face frozen in fear

                  Her pupils dilating
                  More black than brown

  Tears falling backward

            Off her pale porcelain cheeks

                              Too terrified to speak
                              Too scared to squeak

                  Hair capturing her mouth
                  Whipping around

  As she tried to balance on air
  Her arms heavy by the free flowing nothingness

            As she tried to

                        Find something to cling to
                        In the dark of the deepest ditch

February 12, 2021

She gripped onto the cool dirt
Digging her nails deep to get a grip

As she tried to

Climb up from the depths of death
To the land of the living up above

She arched her burning back
Using her strength to do the impossible

Tears falling forwards from
Her pale porcelain cheeks

To create murky mud to suck her hands in deeper

Pulling and pushing her body

Like broken propellers
Running from leftover fumes

She breaks free from the darkness
Lifting higher towards the once lost light

Gripping the grass like a rope

Pulling free from the dark of the deepest ditch

February 14, 2021

She closes her eyes and dreams of forever
Letting her tired eyes search for her heart
In the depths of her brain

Her feet find the crunch
Of dead and blackened rose petals
Sour from a few hours of sitting still
In the dead of night

She tries to call out for her heart
Trying to find it again after so long
Yet her lips found nothing but the putrid stench
Of decade-old chocolates
Falling down her open mouth

Two tears after twelve
And the clock strikes Fourteen
Releasing a battered and bleeding heart

She runs to it, trying to wrap her arms around it
Yet her fingers finding nothing but air
As she sits and waits
Year after year after year

Every point in time
A disappointment
Every reality the same

Until the day the light shone a little brighter
And the roses crunched a little less
And the chocolates made less of a mess
And she jumped a little lighter
To reach her shielded heart

Finding his hands wrapped around hers
Holding her scarred and stitched together heart
Between their entwined fingers
Closing the wounds and keeping her heart secure
Whispering words that did assure
The broken girl she was safe once more
And he was everything she had asked for
The one she did adore
The one she fell for
Evermore

February 15, 2021

Crimson swirls against the canvas
Staining what once was white
Tainting the image of purity
And locking in the pigment
Each particle of paper soaking the color
Into the deep depression of its imperfections

Natural beauty only goes so far
When pain is the motivator

The liquid seeks every surface
Dripping down the pale legs of the stand
Turning what once was brand new into a rusty red
Staining all it seeks
Never minding the emotions of the ones it touches

Red is a warning to never come back again
Yet there is no choice in the matter at hand

Crimson falls so far just to make a statement
Yet the statement is unknown to all, even the artist
For an invisible hand guided
Where the paint must inevitably fall
And the breeze never freezes the paint in place
Always misplaced from where it should be
Natural beauty

February 19, 2021

She sits in a small box the size of her body
Pushing out against the sides
Her chilled fingertips touching
Pressing against the walls
That were pressing in on her
She tried to push with all her strength
Yet the prison didn't even fracture

She sits in a small box the size of her body
Banging out against the sides
Her curled fists brushing
Hitting against the walls
That were hitting against her
She tried to strike with all her strength
Yet the prison didn't even fracture

She sits in a small box the size of her body
Tapping out against the sides
Her long nails beating
Bashing against the walls
That were bashing against her
She tried to jab with all her strength
Yet the prison didn't even fracture

Instead of pushing through the walls
That claimed her as their own
Her heart was pushed to shatter

In the prison that was her chest
Splintering like glass and breaking
Into glittering crimson shards shimmering
In the golden sunlight

And her fists were striked with a million bruises
Scarring from cuts that were inflicted by nothing
But the repeated motion of trying to escape
Broken, bloodied, and barred

And her lips
Tapped of all the words
That could have ever
Flowed
Like an empty maple tree
Drained dry

As all the hope
Was taken away

On that one horrible, no good day

When it felt like happiness was far away

Trapped

                        Just out of reach

Spring

March 1, 2020

Loving is looking to the future
Caring for someone's needs
Hearing their ideas
And loving who they are
Yet it is also looking at the past and seeing
Who they were
And how that made them who they have become
Respecting the road they walked
And the path they chose to see

Love is not sex
Love is not kisses
Love is not the body at all

It's like a Christmas Tree
The tree isn't the ornaments you put on
Or the lights wrapped around it
It isn't the gifts under it
Or the stockings to the side of it
A Christmas Tree is the
Green, Beautiful, Natural plant
And the bark that keeps it standing
Everything else is pretty ornaments
They are nice to have
They make the relationship fun
But they aren't what love is

March 3, 2021

Woman cloaked in red with lips scarred by time
Smiles as she stands at the edge of forever
Her painted nails black but purple all the same
Holding the crown of spikes atop her wretched head

She holds up the final card
Showing the hearts that have since past
Tallying them in the days of last
And speaking them by name

She carves fifty-seven names upon the bark
Of a burned tree ruined by lighting
And adds three of her own names
To the list of the broken hearted

She divides the longest names by the smallest
And rips them into equal parts
Splitting them among the months
And forcing them to guard the people they despised

A cycle complete as time slowly stops

Heart held in open hand
And sacrificed once again
For the sake of the land
A kingdom of creativity

Acknowledgments

Many thanks to everyone who has supported me this year. It has been a tough year for the entire world and probably the Universe as well. In all my struggles I did as I usually do, I used writing as my therapy. I took out my phone, a piece of paper, or even my laptop and took out my frustrations by using the written word. Of course, while I was writing inspiration struck, and a new book idea was born. My book series may have ended with *Daydream* but I never did plan to stop writing. To be quite honest I did not expect to publish a new book, and especially not so soon after the series ended, but I found myself wanting to share these poems with the world. I know deep down that they will speak to more than just my struggles, and in a year where everyone went through so much pain a little bit of love and understanding can go a long way. My hope with this book was to take the pain and turn it into beauty. I hope everyone can feel the emotions and the frustration but that they see the beauty at the end of it all. In my eyes, negativity is only temporary and it opens the windows to reveal the rainbow that was there all along. I want to thank everyone that helped me through this year and showed me my own rainbows. I love you all and happy reading!

Kate Abrielle McCormick is a novice poetry writer from Pennsylvania. She has published works such as "In Her Mind," (2018) "Story In The End," (2019) and "Collection of Voices" (2019). She is currently co-writing the collection titled "Let's Make This Very Queer."

Kate is in her second year at Northampton Community College studying English and Psychology to better her future career as a screenwriter. In 2021, she was an honored speaker for the college as an "influential female writer." She has most of her other work on Amazon, Kindle, Wattpad, Fanfiction.net, Archive of Our Own, and Barnes & Noble.com. Other than writing she enjoys reading, analyzing dreams, and spending time with her family.

Take A Look At Her Other Books

<u>Series</u>
In Her Mind (Book One)
Story in the End (Book Two)
Daydream (Book Three)

<u>Other Books</u>
To Suffer Softly

www.ingramcontent.com/pod-product-compliance
Lightning Source LLC
Chambersburg PA
CBHW071157130726
47998CB00002B/535